URBAN WILDLIFE
Habitats

By **Barbara Taylor**

GARETH**STEVENS**
GS
PUBLISHING
A Member of the WRC Media Family of Companies

Please visit our web site at: www.garethstevens.com
For a free color catalog describing Gareth Stevens Publishing's
list of high-quality books and multimedia programs,
call 1-800-542-2595 or 1-800-387-3178 (Canada).
Gareth Stevens Publishing's fax: (414) 332-3567.

Library of Congress Cataloging-in-Publication Data

Taylor, Barbara, 1954-
  Urban wildlife habitats / Barbara Taylor. – North American ed.
      p. cm. — (Exploring habitats)
  Includes bibliographical references and index.
  ISBN 10: 0-8368-7259-2 – ISBN 13: 978-0-8368-7259-0 (lib. bdg.)
  1. Urban animals—Juvenile literature. I. Title. II. Series.
QL49.T2162   2007
578.75′6—dc22   2006044324

This North American edition first published in 2007 by
Gareth Stevens Publishing
A Member of the WRC Media Family of Companies
330 West Olive Street, Suite 100
Milwaukee, WI 53212 USA

This U.S. edition copyright © 2007 by Gareth Stevens, Inc. Original
edition copyright © 2002 by ticktock Entertainment Ltd. First published
in Great Britain in 1999 by ticktock Publishing Ltd., Unit 2, Orchard
Business Centre, North Farm Road, Tunbridge Wells, Kent, TN2 3XF.

Gareth Stevens editor: Richard Hantula
Gareth Stevens designer: Charlie Dahl
Gareth Stevens managing editor: Mark J. Sachner
Gareth Stevens art direction: Tammy West
Gareth Stevens production: Jessica Morris

Picture Credits: t=top, b=bottom, c=centre, l=left, r=right, OFC=outside
front cover, OBC=outside back cover, IFC=inside front cover

Bruce Coleman Collection; 8/9t, 10b, 11tr, 12/13c, 13b, 14l, 20/21t, 22ct,
24bl, 27tr. Chris Fairclough; 21bl. Heather Angel; 15br, 16/17b, 27bl, 30tl.
Image Bank; 15t, 16cl & 32, 21br, 30bl. NHPA; OFC, 13r. Oxford Scientific
Films; IFC, 2/3t, 2l & OFC, 3br, 3cr, 3t, 4bl, 4tl, 4/5b, 5tr, 5ct, 6l & OBC, 6br,
6/7t, 7tr, 7br, 9tr, 8bl, 9cl, 8tl, 9cr, 10tl, 10/11c, 11cr, 12tl, 14ct, 15c, 16tl,
17tr, 17cr, 17tl, 18/19c, 18/19t, 19c, 19tr, 20bl, 20br, 20tl, 22/23b, 23tr, 23cr,
23br, 24tl, 24/25b, 24/25c, 24/25t, 25br, 27cr, 26t, 26/27c, 29cl, 28bl, 28/29t,
29b, 28tl, 29cr, 29tr, 30/31t, 30br. Survival Anglia; 5tl. Tony Stone Images;
7cr, 18tl & OBC, 22l, 26l, 30cr.

Every effort has been made to trace the copyright holders and we apologize in
advance for any unintentional omissions. We would be pleased to insert the
appropriate acknowledgement in any subsequent edition of this publication.

Printed in the United States of America

1 2 3 4 5 6 7 8 9 10 09 08 07 06

CONTENTS

THE UNEXPECTED VISITOR

Moose (*left*) are probably the largest animals to visit towns in northern regions. Like all urban animals, they are attracted by the promise of food and shelter, expecially during the cold winter.

LIVING ON THE WILD SIDE

Flocks of pigeons fluttering in your face in a city center, the sudden scurrying of a rat along subway tracks, the sound of a mouse scuttling around under the floorboards – these are familiar examples of the wild animals that share our urban environment. And there are many more. Some are visible, many are hidden out of sight, but they all take advantage of the benefits of urban living, such as food the year-round, warmer temperatures in winter months, and a variety of places to shelter and nest. Urban animals have to be adaptable and able to survive constant change, noise, lights, pollution, and disturbance from hordes of people and traffic. Those wild animals that have adapted to the challenges of urban living sometimes exist in large numbers, often becoming pests or health hazards.

ROAD SAFETY

Deciding when to cross a road is a terrifying prospect for many urban animals. Toads setting out to find their breeding ponds in spring often find their migration route blocked by a road (*left*).

HIGH-RISE NESTS

White storks (*left*) normally nest in tall trees, but chimneys, spires, and transmission towers are a good substitute. In some European towns people have built special platforms on their chimneys to act as a base for the huge mass of sticks and other nesting materials that storks use. Storks are supposed to bring good fortune and many children to those people lucky enough to have a nest on their roof, although storks themselves have not been so lucky, as their numbers have been falling.

CATS GONE WILD

In many cities there are staggering populations of feral cats (*left*). These are domestic cats that have been abandoned or made homeless because of war, fire, or floods. Feral cats are independent, secretive, and nocturnal, living in factories, warehouses, sewers, and port areas. They hunt birds, rats, and mice. Without them the problem of urban rats and mice would be more serious.

NESTING SITES

Swallows and swifts often nest on or in buildings, but they were originally cave or cliff dwellers. A swallow's nest is usually supported by a rafter, shelf, or ledge (*right*). The saucer-shaped nest is made from mud and dried grasses, lined with feathers and bits of plants. Swallows also rest on artificial perches, such as telegraph poles and wires, rather than natural perches, such as trees.

SUPER SURVIVORS

Rats and mice thrive in the hearts of the largest and dirtiest cities around the world. Thousands of brown rats (*left*) live beneath our feet in sewers, drains, and other underground tunnels. Black rats originally lived in trees and like to climb. They make their homes aboveground in roof and loft spaces. Rats and mice first spread to urban habitats by traveling on ships from one port to another.

POPULAR PIGEONS?

Like swallows, pigeons are rock- and cliff-dwelling birds that now make their homes on the artificial cliffs of our cities. One of the reasons for their spectacular success as an urban animal is that they can breed year-round. Some people like pigeons so much that they feed them (*right*) – although not always from their own mouths! In Roman times, pigeons were so highly regarded that bread given to them had to first be chewed by slaves. Today, they cause problems in towns owing to the mess they make and the diseases they carry.

GARDEN PEST

Rabbits such as the eastern cottontail (*above*) have become pests in some parts of North America, eating away at garden plants and digging up flowerbeds. They are difficult to catch because their large, mobile ears help them detect danger, and their long legs are adapted for fast running. They are good at burrowing and gnawing and often find a way through rabbit-proof fencing.

NORTH AND SOUTH AMERICAN CITIES

From the cold, snowy wastes of Canada to the subtropical or tropical warmth of Florida or Brazil, a variety of wild animals have made their homes in the cities of the Americas. Polar bears scavenge in garbage dumps in sub-Arctic Canadian towns, while moose sometimes leave the forests and wander through the streets. Peregrine falcons nest on skyscrapers in Los Angeles, caimans live in Florida canals, and raccoons are common where there is plenty of garbage. In some South American cities, house mice with very thick fur survive in refrigerated stores. But American cities also have lots of the most common city birds – the house, or English, sparrow; the rock pigeon ("rock dove"); and the European starling. These are not native birds but were introduced at different times – rock pigeons in the 17th century, house sparrows between 1850 and 1870, and starlings in 1890-91, when a flock of 100 birds were released in New York City's Central Park. Today, there are over 200 million starlings in North America.

DEER LUNCH

Some wapiti, or American elks, seem to find playing fields an ideal spot for a rest and a grassy lunch (*right*). Urban areas can provide animals like these with safe refuges from hunters, although such large mammals are not common in towns.

SUN-BATHING SLOTH

A colony of sloths lives in a city park in Santa Cruz, Bolivia. Sloths regulate their body temperature by moving in and out of the Sun, and this one (*left*) seems to be enjoying the sunshine. It is not frightened of being so close to humans. When wild animals are fed regularly by people, they can become very tame.

PEREGRINE PERCHES

Downtown areas are ideal for peregrine falcons (*right*) because the tall buildings there are just like the rocky cliffs on which they like to breed. There are also lots of pigeons to eat. In the United States many young birds bred in captivity have been introduced into cities such as Washington D.C., Baltimore, Cincinnati, Cleveland, and Los Angeles. Humans act as surrogate parents, overseeing and feeding the birds until they can look after themselves. About a dozen chicks need to be released over two years to ensure one breeding pair. Dangers such as plateglass windows and wires cause the death of eight out of ten of the young birds.

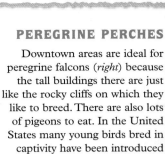

HAPPY HUMMERS

Hummingbirds have no fear of people, so they have no problem living in cities. People in North America often hang hummingbird feeders in their back yards because they enjoy watching the tiny birds (*left*). Inside the feeders is a sugary liquid, rather like the nectar hummingbirds take from flowers. Sugar is a good food for hummingbirds because it can be turned into energy very quickly and hummingbirds need a lot of instant energy to keep their tiny bodies warm.

SKUNK STINK

In some American towns, skunks (*below*) emerge after dusk to scavenge for food. A skunk's bold black-and-white stripes carry a warning that no one can afford to ignore. To defend itself, a skunk squirts out a nasty-smelling, amber-colored liquid from glands on its hind end. People who get this liquid on their clothes while trying to chase a skunk off their property will want to consider throwing the clothes awas the odor is difficult to remove. A folk remedy is to use tomato juice, but it, at best, only masks the smell.

SPINY VISITOR

The European hedgehog (*below right*) finds suburban gardens very similar to its natural habitat of woodland edges. Gardens offer the same sort of food, such as worms, slugs, snails, beetles, and caterpillars, as well as leaves and grasses for nesting material. But urban hedgehogs face a lot of hazards, among them pesticides, ponds with smooth sides that may be impossible to climb out of, and the possibility someone may start a fire atop a hibernating hedgehog.

FEATHERED HUNTERS

For owls, such as the ghostly white barn owl (*left*), the tawny owl, and the little owl, the many rodents scurrying about towns provide an easy meal. Barn owls have even nested in the belfry of the cathedral of Notre Dame in Paris, France. The snoring and hissing of barn owl fledglings in church towers may have been partly responsible for stories of ghosts and goblins roaming about churchyards at night.

GRAY INVADERS

What Europeans call the gray squirrel (*above*) is a North American species – the eastern gray squirrel – that was initally introduced into Britain around the beginning of the 20th century. Numerous additional introductions followed, leading to a population explosion of gray squirrels and the gradual decline of the native red squirrel. Gray squirrels love to chew and can cause serious problems if they nest in loft spaces or get inside houses.

EUROPEAN CITIES

Europe is a busy place. In many of its countries, large numbers of people are crowded into noisy towns and cities. The climate is generally temperate, becoming icy cold in the far north and warmer in the south. Moose have wandered into snowy Moscow, not very far from Red Square, yet in some towns in southern France, the buzzing of semitropical cicadas fills the air. Some urban animals have spread eastward from Europe to other parts of the world. Rabbits and starlings, for example, to Australia. Others have moved in the opposite direction – collared doves spread across Europe from Istanbul, and brown rats traveled west from their haunts in Russia. European scavenger birds, such as kites and ravens, have all but disappeared as sanitary conditions have improved. There is, however, still one famous band of ravens kept at the Tower of London; their wings are clipped to keep them from flying away. Legend has it that if they leave, the tower and the kingdom will fall.

PIGEON ESCAPES

The hordes of rock pigeons that are at home in all cities, from London's Trafalgar Square (*above*) to the Blue Mosque (*below*) in Mazar-e Sharif, Afghanistan, are actually feral birds, the now wild descendants of domesticated pigeons that were reared as a source of food. The birds were initially domesticated in Iraq over 6,000 years ago. Some city pigeons may also have come from racing pigeons that strayed or became lost. Feral pigeons are remarkably variable in color and markings, partly because of breeding and partly as an adaptation to the town environment. Dark-colored birds may survive better in colder climates, since dark colors absorb the Sun's warmth. Lighter-colored birds stay cooler in warmer climates, as light colors reflect the heat.

BUTTERFLY BONANZA

The butterfly bush, *Buddleja davidii*, was introduced from China to Europe and North America as a garden shrub about 100 years ago. Now it thrives on town building sites and wasteland, as well as in town gardens. Its flowers are extremely attractive to 20 or more species of butterflies, including peacock butterflies (*right*), as well as other nectar-feeding insects, such as hoverflies and bumble bees.

SCARY SPIDERS

The Sydney funnel-web spider (*above*) is one of the most dangerous spiders in the world. It lives within about 100 miles (160 kilometers) of the center of Sydney, Australia. Females rarely move far from their burrows but may bite people while they are gardening or gathering logs. Males sometimes enter houses in summer when searching for females and may crawl into shoes or clothing left on the floor. Both sexes are very aggressive, and their massive fangs can go through a child's fingernail.

ASIAN AND AUSTRALIAN CITIES

The urban animals of southern Asia and Australia are drawn to the cities by opportunities for shelter and excellent supplies of food. In India, certain animals, such as cows and monkeys, are venerated and protected for religious reasons, while jackals, vultures, and kites scavenge for leftovers. Some house guests, such as the house gecko, are welcome for clearing the rooms of insect pests. Geckos are also considered lucky animals. Others, such as deadly poisonous spiders and snakes are widely feared. Australian city wildlife is dominated by marsupials, such as possums nesting in lofts. There are also a number of urban species that were introduced to Australia from Europe, such as starlings, sparrows, and rabbits. Foxes, stoats, and weasels were introduced in the 19th century to combat a rabbit plague. They failed to stop the rabbits but are still living in Australia today.

POSSUM LODGERS

In Australian cities, such as Sydney and Melbourne, cat-sized common brushtail possums have invaded homes in considerable numbers. They get into attics, where they sometimes rip up ceilings to set up home. The possums also raid trash bins and bird feeders in suburban gardens. This mother and young (*right*) are nesting in a boarded-up fireplace.

TEMPLE MONKEYS

Monkeys, such as these (*left*) sitting on the Monkey Temple in Kathmandu, Nepal, are treated well by Hindus because of the Hindu monkey god, Hanuman. In the ancient Sanskrit epic called the Ramayana, the monkey chieftain Hanuman helps Rama (an incarnation of the god Vishnu) recover his wife, who was abducted by the demon king Ravana. There are probably more monkeys living in the cities in India than in the forests.

SACRED COWS

Cows are allowed to wander freely through the streets of Indian cities and even raid vegetable stands (*right*). Hindus respect animal life and believe that when we hurt living things, we hurt ourselves. Many Hindus are vegetarians. They also think of cows, which give people milk to drink, as mothers, and they never eat beef.

MEGABATS

Fruit bats (*left*) have furry, foxlike faces and so are also called flying foxes. They roost in trees during the day, sometimes stripping away leaves so members of their colony can see each other more clearly. At dusk they leave their roosts in search of food. In cities such as Sydney, they feed on fig trees in the city parks at night and are often heard making harsh, squealing noises.

STREETWISE KANGAROO

Hopping along a street in Queensland, Australia (*right*), are a mother and joey (baby) eastern gray kangaroo. The mother has only one baby at a time, and the joey leaves the pouch when it is about ten months old. Beginning in the late 18th century, human settlement markedly altered kangaroos' original habitat, forcing the animals to compete for grazing land and cope with predators, such as domestic cats, dogs, and European red foxes.

AFRICAN CITIES

TAME BIRD

The African pied wagtail (*above*) is a very tame and confiding bird that is closely associated with human dwellings. It lives in pairs or small groups and has a pleasant warbling song rather like that of a canary. This wagtail nests in holes in buildings and river banks, laying three eggs with many pale, yellowish-brown markings.

Temperatures in African cities are generally high, night and day, except in a few mountainous areas. Rainfall varies a good deal, from the dry, arid northern cities, such as Cairo, Egypt, to the wet, lush southern cities, such as Cape Town, South Africa. European starlings were first introduced into Africa in Cape Town, supposedly by the 19th-century South African businessman and statesman Cecil Rhodes. They proceeded to rapidly expand their range. There are also tropical birds, such as weaverbirds scavenging for leftovers and sunbirds flitting about parks and gardens. Geckos fulfil a useful role eating insects in buildings, but one, the lobe-footed gecko, used to be regarded with unnecessary dread in Egyptian towns; it was known as "the father of leprosy." Termites can also be bad news because of the damage they cause to wooden buildings. African city mammals include rats and monkeys, which can be a considerable nuisance.

CAMP FOLLOWER

This African elephant (*left*) has wandered into a tourist camp in the Masai Mara National Reserve in Kenya. Elephants are intelligent animals, and they soon learn that human camps are useful sources of extra food or water. Sometimes camps are built across traditional migration routes of elephants. Because they are such huge animals, they are difficult to keep out of the camps and may cause damage with their huge bulk. For the tourists, the chance to get really close to a wild elephant is an amazing experience. Other game animals can also get too close for comfort. In 1898-99, the man-eating lions of Tsavo stopped all work on the Mombasa to Uganda railroad when workers refused to continue unless they were protected. The lions killed as many as 135 men before they were finally shot.

ROOFTOP MONKEYS

Colobus monkeys are good climbers and jumpers – their long hair and tail serve as parachutes when they leap. In the forests they rarely descend to the ground, so climbing onto this Kenyan rooftop (*right*) must have been easy for them. They may be looking for leaves to eat in the garden around the house.

VULTURE DUTY

Stalking about with their characteristic goose step, Egyptian vultures (*above*) search for morsels of food among the town and city rubbish dumps of North, Central, and East Africa. These vultures also feed on human excrement. The Egyptian vulture is one of the few tool-using birds, breaking eggs by throwing stones at them.

GAS STATION ATTENDANT

This yellow baboon (*left*) looks as if it is waiting to sell a customer some gasoline. It may be waiting for a car to arrive, hoping for a free snack. The yellow baboon is a large, slender animal, often measuring over 3 feet (1 meter) long, not counting the tail; it has conspicuously long legs. It comes out during the day and lives in groups.

THE ULTIMATE URBAN ANIMAL

AMERICAN FOXES

This red fox (*above*) has set up home in a Colorado cemetery. In North America urban red foxes have to compete with raccoons, coyotes, bobcats, and even cougars. They have not become as familiar urban animals as they have in countries such as Britain.

Red foxes are common worldwide. They are widespread and numerous in urban Britain, but also live in other cities of Europe, Australia, and North America. Foxes have adapted well to city living because they are not very fussy about where they live or what they eat. They are small enough to be unobtrusive, yet large enough to travel long distances in search of food. Some foxes are commuters, coming into town only at night to eat. Urban areas provide foxes with refuge from hunters and traps. Other urban members of the dog family include dingoes, jackals, and coyotes.

TRACKING FOXES

To build up a picture of the number of foxes in towns and cities and how they move about, scientists study their tracks and droppings.

FOX: FRONT FOOT   **FOX: BACK FOOT**   **DOG**

Fox footprints are like those of a small dog, only narrower. Claw marks are usually clearly visible.

FRESH (DARK)

DRY (WHITE)

Fox droppings are about 3-4 inches (7-10 centimeters) long. They look like dog droppings but have a twisted point at one end. They are usually dark and may be made up of bits of mice, birds, hard parts of insects, fruit, and berries. Older droppings become paler and much more brittle.

DINGO DOGS

The original dingo was a primitive dog probably descended from the Indian wolf. It was spread through East Asia by traders and travelers and apparently arrived in Australia some 4,000–6,000 years ago. Today's dingoes breed freely with feral dogs, and few pure dingo populations remain. Dingoes scavenge on rubbish heaps (*above*) but have a wide and varied diet.

CITY COYOTE

In some western U.S. cites coyotes (*right*) have adapted well to urban life. They are particularly common in Los Angeles, where they hide in scrub-filled ravines during the day and move into built-up areas to feed at night. Coyotes can breed with domestic dogs to produce "coydogs," which are more likely to attack domestic animals, such as cats, dogs, and chickens. Coyotes have even attacked people, which is one thing that urban foxes never do.

Adult foxes molt their fur once each year, between spring and midsummer. While molting, they often look scruffy, thin, and long-legged. In winter they grow thick, warm coats.

Most urban foxes lead short lives – 55 percent die in their first year and 80 percent die before they are three years old. A few dominant, and lucky, animals may survive to live and breed for up to eight years.

Foxes are relatively small animals, only a little heavier than a pet cat.

Touch-sensitive whiskers and hairs on the muzzle, around the eyes, and under the chin help the fox to find its way through vegetation or explore new runs or holes.

Foxes have keen enough hearing to detect the rustling noises made by voles and other rodents as they move.

Foxes have 42 teeth, including four sharp, pointed canines to kill and tear prey, and carnassial teeth in the side of the mouth for cutting food.

FOX SPEAK

To most city dwellers, it is the eerie, blood-chilling screams of foxes (*left*) in the middle of the night that are most familiar. It is generally the vixens (females) that scream, while the dog (male) foxes bark. These strange noises can be heard at any time of year but are more common in January, when foxes are mating.

DAYTIME VISITORS

MOLE MOUNTAINS

Moles can make a real mess of a grassy lawn in a garden or town park, and they are very difficult to get rid of. The molehills we see on the ground (*above*) are waste soil that they push aboveground as they dig their tunnels. Most of their food comes from soil animals, such as worms that fall into their tunnels. In places where food is scarce, moles have to dig more burrows and push up more molehills to find enough food to eat.

Different urban animals are active by day and by night. This helps them to share the resources of the urban habitat and avoid competition. Daytime creatures, such as squirrels, are the ones we are most likely to notice, although the night is usually a busier time because most of the humans are out of the way. People are the biggest nuisance for urban animals. They swat houseflies, flick away the cobwebs of house spiders, and chase squirrels and wasps away from their picnics. The residents of Tokyo, Japan, swatted about 117 million houseflies on National Fly Day in 1933. People also prevent larger animals from getting in the way of their daily lives, by building fences around their golf courses or culling animal populations if they become a problem. But one of the reasons that urban animals survive is that they are not easily frightened by people.

SUPERMARKET SHOPPER

This great egret (*left*) has no intention of paying for its food at the checkout of this Florida supermarket. Instead, it has spotted a few meat scraps lying about and has moved in to claim a free meal. Great egrets usually feed in swamps and marshes, stalking fish, frogs, snakes, and crayfish in shallow water. As people have invaded its natural habitat, the bird has been forced to change some of its feeding habits.

KANGAROO GOLFERS

These kangaroos (*right*) have taken advantage of an empty Australian golf course to grab a tasty grass snack. It is difficult to make such areas kangaroo-proof, since kangaroos are good at jumping fences and can leap up to 10 feet (3 m) in height and 30 feet (9 m) in length. Normally, kangaroos graze during the night and rest up in the shade during the day.

FREE FOOD

Gray squirrels (*right*) will eat almost anything, from garden bulbs, fish, honey, and fruit to fungi, carrion (dead flesh), and young birds and their eggs. They take full advantage of any free samples people leave out for them. Gray squirrels are agile and alert animals with a good sense of smell and very good eyesight. They spend a good deal of time foraging on the ground and have to be always ready to spring into the trees at the first sign of danger.

STRIPED ANGEL

People are usually afraid of wasps because they can sting, but they are in fact very beneficial insects. For most of the summer they hunt insect pests in the garden and are far too busy getting food for their young to bother us. At the end of the summer, a wasp colony begins to break up. The workers have no more young to feed and start to turn their attention to fruit and other sweet substances. This is when the wasps can be annoying, but as soon as the weather turns cold, they die. Only mated queens survive the winter.

A NIGHT ON THE TOWN

BADGER VISIT

Badgers, (*above*) particularly European badgers, often visit towns for food, but more because the town has spread into their bit of countryside than because they have moved into town. They need open space and peace and quiet and are not as adaptable as many urban animals, except in their diet. Badgers eat many things. They love earthworms but will also eat carrion, insects, small mammals and birds, fruit, vegetables, and seeds. They have even been seen crunching glass bottles and chewing on golf balls.

As the sun sets and people settle down inside their homes for the night, a whole new group of animals emerge from their daytime hiding places. Animal sounds – the hoot of an owl, the snuffling of a badger, the rustling of a raccoon, the fluttering of a moth, or the scream of a fox – are easier to hear at night because there is less traffic noise. Many small animals find it easier to hide from their enemies in the darkness. Nighttime animals have keen senses, especially hearing and smell, to help them search for food or mates or detect danger. Animals that lose water easily, such as slugs, snails, and wood lice, prefer to come out at night because the air is cooler and damper. In some countries in the spring, a striking dawn chorus ends the night, as the birds sing to lay claim to their nesting territory.

SUPER MICE

House mice (*left*) can live almost anywhere – in coal mines, subway stations, or even frozen-meat stores. They have good eyesight and a particularly good sense of smell. They can also run fast, which is possibly the best defense against their biggest predator – the cat. House mice usually live in extended families feauring a dominant male, his harem of females, and several generations of offspring. One female mouse can have about 25 young in a year. As well as eating our food, mice can be a problem because they spread diseases and may even set off burglar alarms as they patter around houses at night.

LUCKY GECKOS

In tropical countries the sound of a gecko in the bedroom at night is a welcome one because it is there to catch insects (*right*). The gecko is the only reptile with a true voice. In Bangkok, Thailand, it is thought to be an especially good sign if a gecko happens to be uttering its cry when a baby is born. Geckos have suction pads under their toes to help them scurry up and down walls; they even walk upside down across the ceiling.

TOAD TRAVELER

In 1935 some 62,000 South American cane toads (*left*) were released in Queensland, Australia, in an attempt to control sugarcane pests. The toads spread to many other areas, including residential ones, and began to eat useful creatures, such as geckos and small frogs. The cane toads have proved too successful, since they eat almost anything, produce vast numbers of eggs (up to 30,000 eggs per clutch), and do not have any serious predators in Australia. At night they can often be seen sitting under streetlights or garden lights, plucking flying insects out of the air.

BATTY SUPERSTITIONS

Despite their image of mystery and sinister happenings, bats are in fact unobtrusive and inoffensive animals, glad to avoid their human neighbors. They prefer to roost in modern, clean houses rather than dusty, drafty old ones. They are scrupulously clean and usually quiet and nonsmelly. Long-eared bats (*right*) have the longest ears relative to their body size of any mammal. They use their sensitive ears to pick up the echoes of high-pitched sounds they make. This is called "echolocation" and helps most bats navigate and find food.

CITIZEN RACCOON

The streetwise raccoon (*left*) not only tolerates people but seems to thrive in dense human settlements such as towns and cities in North America. Generally shy by nature, raccoons time their visits for the hours when humans are fewer, garbage is fresher, and bird feeders are fully stocked. They may build their dens in chimneys or drains, which are like the hollow branches or tree trunks in which they nest in the wild. Raccoons succeed at urban life because they are secretive, adaptable, and able to make a meal out of most natural and artificial city foodstuffs. A city can also be a refuge for raccoons, as they may be trapped and hunted in the countryside.

ANIMAL LODGERS

The artificial habitats in our homes are similar to many natural ones – walls are like cliffs, attics and cellars are like caves, chimney pipes are like tall trees, and wooden furniture is like fallen logs in a forest. Even though we may not be aware of it, our homes may be full of uninvited guests (*left*). Some can cause problems by carrying diseases or damaging our homes and the things in them. Others, such as spiders and geckos, are useful because they eat unwanted insects.

COCKROACH SURVIVAL

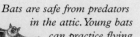

Cockroaches (*below*) are mainly tropical insects that have traveled all over the world with people. They probably could not survive in cooler countries outside towns and cities. Cockroaches are active at night and spend the day hidden in warm places, such as ovens or radiators, although they have been found in televisions, clocks, and telephones and on the backs of refrigerators. They eat almost anything, including glue, paper, soap, shoe polish, and ink and can exist without food for up to three months. Cockroaches have to keep clean to preserve their waxy coating, which keeps them from drying out in centrally heated homes. But they can spread bacteria that are harmful to humans.

BATS

Bats are safe from predators in the attic. Young bats can practice flying there, too.

Wasps may hang their paper nests from attic beams.

WASPS

SWALLOWS

Swallows may nest under the eaves of houses.

SPIDERS

Spiders are useful house guests, as they stalk, snare, and ambush insects for breakfast, lunch, and dinner.

Woodworm beetle larvae can reduce furniture to dust.

WOODWORM

GECKOS

Houseflies visit garbage, dead animals, and dung and can carry diseases.

HOUSEFLIES

Dog and cat fleas suck the animals blood and bite humans, too.

FLEAS

Geckos cling to walls and ceilings and hunt insects.

Silverfish are often found in kitchens, searching for sugary and starchy foods.

SILVERFISH

House mice live in attics, under floors, and in gaps in brickwork, gnawing through wooden partitions to find food.

HOUSE MICE

FOXES

Foxes may nest in cellars or under floorboards.

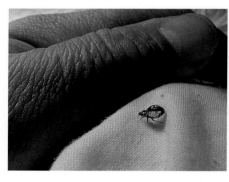

BITING BUGS

Bedbugs (*above*) are about ¼ inch (6 millimeters) long and are big enough to see easily. They jab their piercing mouthparts into a victim in search of blood. In about ten minutes an adult bedbug can suck up to seven times its weight in blood. In human beings each jab of a bedbug leaves a red, itchy spot. Bedbugs probably came originally from Asia but have now spread to all parts of the world. They need a warm, dry climate, and they spread to northern parts of the world once buildings started to be well heated.

HOUSE PARTY

Did you know that about a million dust mites live in an ordinary single bed? Or that book lice feed on the tiny molds that grow on the pages of books or under wallpaper? These are just two of the many creatures that lurk unseen in the hidden corners of our homes – on walls or in wardrobes, carpets, curtains, and kitchen cupboards. Many of them are tiny, or even microscopic, but a few, such as bats in the attic or mice under the floorboards, are larger, noisier, and more obvious. Some of them would once have lived in caves or big holes in trees but prefer the warmth of our homes, with their built-in food supply. The larvae of many moths and beetles munch their way through our food, clothes, curtains, and carpets. They include clothes moths, meal moths, flour beetles, larder beetles, leather beetles, grain weevils, and carpet beetles. Some of these insects find their way into our homes from the nests of birds, rodents, and wasps that are built in and around human habitations.

DUST FOR DINNER

Billions of microscopic dust mites (*above*) chomp away on the bits of dead skin that flake off our bodies. Much of the dust in our homes is made up of human skin! Dust mites are so small you cannot see them, and no one knew they existed until the 1960s. Some people are allergic to dust mite droppings. They sniff and sneeze and even get asthma if they breathe in too many of them.

TASTY CLOTHES

The larvae of clothes moths (*right*) feed on anything made from animal or plant fibers, such as woolens, silks, and cottons. They will also feed on flour, meat, and dead insects. Clothes moths originally came from warmer parts of the world and do not live outside in cooler, temperate countries. They have been decreasing because of increased use of synthetic materials in clothes, improvements in home cleaning, and advances in heating that make our homes drier.

YUMMY CARPETS

Carpet beetle larvae (*left*) are covered with hairs, so they are sometimes called woolly bears. They feed on woolen textiles, hair, feathers, and even foodstuffs. Adult females lay their eggs in places where there will be food for the larvae. In the wild, the eggs are laid in the nests of mice and birds. Adults fly around outside during the summer and feed on nectar and pollen. They often find their way indoors.

ON THE ROAD

The roads that crisscross our towns and cities can be useful as corridors, allowing animals to move from one area to another. They can also provide feeding grounds for insects and small seed-eating birds as well as hunting birds such as kestrels and owls, or scavengers such as crows, magpies, and jackdaws. But, on the whole, they are polluted and dangerous barriers to animals, especially slow-moving ones, such as toads that need to cross roads to reach their breeding ponds, or low-flying birds, such as blackbirds. Badgers suffer badly, too, because roads may cut across the traditional tracks they follow from burrow to burrow. The usual defenses of many animals are useless against cars and trucks – hedgehogs roll up into a ball and rely on their spines for protection; deer and rabbits freeze if they think running is too risky. Sometimes animals are protected by people who set up special crossing points on roads.

ANIMAL CROSSINGS

Specially designed signs (*below*) aim to draw drivers' attention to the possibility of animals on the road, rather like warning signs near schools that show children. The hope is that drivers will slow down and take more care when they see the signs. In some countries people sometimes stand by the side of a road to help toads cross it safely as they migrate to their breeding grounds at night.

RAMBLING KOALA

This koala (*above*) has not chosen a good spot for watching the traffic. Although Australia's koalas spend much of their time in the trees, they often come to the ground, where they can run nimbly. They are also excellent swimmers. Koalas usually stay within an area of 7–10 acres (3–4 hectares), but rambles of 20 miles (30 km) or so have been recorded.

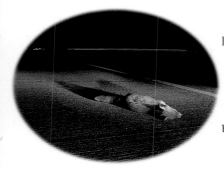

ROADKILL

This fox (*left*) is a victim of a speeding car. Snakes are often killed when they come out to lie on a warm road surface. Every driver is familiar with the sight of animals flattened on the road or lying battered on the shoulder. Even if an animal is only hurt, it may die later from the shock of the accident or be too badly injured to survive in the wild.

TURTLE TRUCK

With an enormous truck speeding toward it only a few yards away, a slow-moving turtle (*right*) has little chance of making it safely across the road. Its strong shell was not designed to withstand such a powerful crushing force. Some turtles live both in water and on land and eat both plants and animals.

THE CLEANUP CREWS

From household trash left outside our homes to garbage left on the streets or dumped in large landfill sites, the food we throw away feeds a surprising variety of urban animals and winged scavengers. Bacterial decomposition of the garbage releases warmth, and this attracts indoor scavengers, such as cockroaches and house crickets, as well as mice in the winter. Reptiles such as certain snakes and lizards may also exploit the internal warmth of a garbage dump. The myriad of trash-dwelling invertebrates (animals without a backbone) includes dung flies, bluebottles, houseflies, hoverflies, owl midges, spiders, bees, earthworms, roundworms, and springtails. All these creatures act as natural recyclers, making good use of the things we throw away.

TRASH RATS

Rats (*left*) thrive in the dirtiest parts of town, which include garbage dumps. Rats in the Italian city of Pisa were once deprived of their staple diet by the installation of a new waste incinerator. They responded by swarming into the city center, leaving only when trash was delivered from a neighboring town. Rats are intelligent, cunning survivors, but they cause immense damage in towns, as well as spreading diseases.

GREEDY GULLS

The harsh sound of gulls squabbling over juicy bits of garbage is a noisy reminder of the important role scavengers play in the natural world. These gulls (*left*) have turned their back on the sea and now spend most of the year feeding at garbage dumps instead. They migrate to the coast only to breed. Gulls are tough and aggressive and find rich pickings among the trash. Some species even steal from other gulls. In Europe, common (mew) gulls get most of their food by robbing black-headed gulls.

BEAR VISITORS

In the autumn large numbers of polar bears pass by Churchill, a town in Manitoba, Canada, on their way to their hunting grounds far out over the frozen ice covering Hudson Bay. The bears are hungry after spending summer on land, where there are no seals for them to hunt. They find the town garbage dump particularly attractive (*right*). The bears are a serious hazard to the people of Churchill, however, since they are very strong and unpredictable.

SCAVENGER STORK

Marabou storks of Africa need more than of 25 ounces (700 grams) of food each day, most of which they obtain by scavenging. They are often attracted to more than garbage dumps, and they also scavenge at lion kills, where they compete with vultures and hyenas for food. Their size and large bills help them steal bits of food from nearby vultures. Here (*right*) they are joined by some baboons that are hoping to find an easy meal.

RACCOON PROOF?

A raccoon (*left*) is able to defeat most attempts to make garbage cans raccoon proof, since it has dexterous front paws that can even unscrew lids or pull tops from bottles. The animals have been known to unlatch a door, walk into a kitchen, open a refrigerator, and help themselves to the contents.

WOOLLY RECYCLERS

People do throw away an awful lot of food, which makes a tasty free meal for many animals. These Welsh sheep (*right*) may not be the most common visitors to garbage dumps, but they are helping to recycle some of the waste we produce. This is useful, as there is too much trash and not enough places for it to go. Trash can contain sharp or broken objects, however, that can injure animals and people sorting through the leftovers.

Even though many towns and cities are built near rivers and streams, it is often the artificial waterways of canals, reservoirs, old gravel pits, and park or garden ponds that are more useful for wildlife. Reservoirs are particularly important as wintering grounds for migrating wildfowl. Slow-moving canal waters shelter pond creatures, such as frogs, water striders, water voles, and moorhens. Bridges and other structures along canals provide roosting sites for bats. Ponds are fascinating miniature ecosystems for a variety of invertebrates, as well as frogs, newts, and fish. Larger animals such as foxes and hedgehogs may drink from them. Spectacular, jewel-like kingfishers are also sometimes glimpsed along waterways right in the middle of towns.

SPINNING BEETLES

On the surface of still or slow-flowing waters, shiny whirligig beetles (*above*) spin gracefully in small groups. Most of their legs are flattened and fringed with hairs for swimming. The eyes are divided into two parts: the top part for seeing in the air and the bottom part for seeing underwater. Adult whirligig beetles feed mainly on insects that have fallen onto the surface of the water. To survive low winter temperatures, the whirligigs bury themselves in the mud.

EXTRA FOOD

Waterfowl in towns and cities, such as swans (*right*), benefit from the extra food people bring for them. But they can also be harmed by polluted waters or injured by rubbish, such as cans and plastic bags. Swans sometimes die after becoming entangled in fishing lines or by swallowing lead fishing-line weights. The lead slowly poisons the swans. Nontoxic alternatives to lead sinkers and better riverbank behavior by fishermen have saved many swans from this unpleasant fate.

SLOW MOVER

Unlike most water snails, which eat only plants, the great pond snail (*left*) also eats decaying animals, fish eggs, and even small fish. It is common in large ponds in Britain and Europe and has also become established in Australia, Asia, Canada, and the middle states of the United States. Great pond snails can obtain oxygen from the air using a simple lung, and remain submerged for long periods in well-oxygenated waters.

MOSQUITO EMERGENCE

Mosquito larvae must live in water, whether it is a pond or a metal can full of water. Sometimes called "wigglers" or "wrigglers," they hang upside down from the surface of the water, breathing air through a tube. Eventually, they turn into pupae, which stretch out on the surface when the adult is ready to emerge. The adult stretches upward until the ends of its long legs slip out of the pupa and its body can drop forward onto the surface film of the water (*right*). After resting for a short time, the mosquito flies away. Only females suck blood – they need a meal of blood before they can lay their eggs. Males are nectar feeders.

SHY FROG

Adult frogs (*right*) are very shy and leap into the water at the first sign of danger. Their long, streamlined shape and powerful back legs with webbed toes help them to swim fast. Frogs mate and lay their eggs in the water. The eggs are surrounded by a jelly substance that helps keep them warm and protects them from damage caused by other animals or the movement of the water. The eggs hatch into tiny tadpoles, which have no legs and breathe through gills. Eventually, the tadpoles develop into frogs, with legs and lungs, and hop out of the water onto land.

NEWT DANCE

In spring the male great crested newt (*left*) develops a high, ragged crest along his back and tail and turns orange-red underneath. He produces secretions from special glands to attract a mate. The female lays up to 300 eggs, which she wraps individually in the leaves of water plants. When seized, the newt gives off a bad-tasting fluid.

Changes in the food supply or seasonal changes in weather may force some urban animals to embark on remarkable migration journeys. One swallow record breaker flew from Johannesburg, South Africa, to Leninsk-Kuznetsky, Russia, a distance of some 7,500 miles (12,000 km), in just 34 days. Other urban visitors, such as moose, wander over much smaller distances, but their journeys are also based on the need to find food. Fruit bats of the tropics make regular mass migrations to find ripe fruit. Migrating animals find their way by using instinctive knowledge, physical landmarks, Earth's magnetic field, sounds, smells, and the positions of the Sun, Moon, and stars in the sky.

FRUITFUL SEARCH

Most fruit bats (*above*) live in large colonies. In Kampala, Uganda, hundreds of thousands of bats hang from trees during the daytime. Fruit bats often migrate in search of ripening fruit. For instance, the gray-headed fruit bat of Australia moves about in search of wild figs. Australian fruitbats, or flying foxes, migrate periodically from Queensland to New South Wales, often doing considerable damage to fruit trees in northern and eastern Australia. Fruit bats also migrate to South Africa during the southern summer and fly northward down the Nile in the rainy season.

ROUTE CHANGES

People have radically changed the migration habits of the Canada goose (*left*), which used to breed in the Alaskan summer and fly south to the Gulf of Mexico for the winter. Now many geese remain in city parks all year round. Thousands of wintering geese also remain in wildlife refuges in the central United States, rather than flying farther south. Geese can cause hygiene problems in parks because of the huge amount of waste they produce. A flock of 300 geese can produce a ton of waste in four days.

CAN SOMEONE TAKE MY ORDER?

This moose (*right*) has obviously taken a liking to fast food! During warmer seasons moose follow a nomadic lifestyle, wandering over a vast expanse of country and sometimes ending up in cities. In the winter they tend to collect together and retire to some sheltered area, where they remain until warmer weather returns in the spring. The promise of food may also draw them to cities in the winter.

SOARING STORKS

White storks (*left*) migrate from Europe to Africa to avoid the cold European winter, returning year after year to their favorite chimneys and rooftops to build their enormous nests. Migrating flocks of storks – sometimes hundreds strong – are a spectacular sight on their autumn migrations as they soar on thermals (columns of warm air) rising over cities such as Istanbul, in Turkey, and Gibraltar, at the southern tip of Spain. They will not fly over large expanses of water where there are no thermals on which they can glide.

SWALLOW SURVIVAL

European swallows (*right*) spend half their year in Europe and half in Africa. In the autumn they leave behind winter's cold weather and shortage of insect food and fly south to a relatively warm and safe environment in Africa. In spring they fly north again to Europe, where there are long hours of daylight and an abundance of food – two advantages when rearing their young. On their migration journeys swallows may cover as much as 190 miles (300 km) a day and reach speeds in the neighborhood of 45 miles (70 km) an hour.

HITCHHIKERS

Some urban animals do not make their journeys by choice. They are carried around the world on ships or planes accidentally. This tree frog (*left*) might very well find itself transported to a new home on a ship, if the bananas on which it sits are shipped from a tropical country to a cooler one. Spiders are often transported in this way. They also travel with bunches of grapes, because they may be busy feeding on grape pests when the grapes are harvested.

PAPER NEST

Wasps build wonderful nests of papier-mâché, which is made by the wasps themselves from chewed-up wood. The paper nest (*above*) consists of eight or more layers of six-sided cells, which are joined to the layers above by pillars of paper. Eggs laid by the queen wasp in the cells will hatch into worker wasps. She has to glue the eggs into the cells to keep them from falling out. At the end of the summer, workers make larger "royal cells" in which to rear new queens. The whole nest is covered with several layers of wasp paper.

NESTS, EGGS, AND YOUNG

Birds, insects, frogs, toads, snakes, and mammals all find safe places to build their nests and raise their young in our homes, gardens, parks, and office buildings. The fact that some people put out food for town and city creatures is a real bonus for busy parents struggling to fill the ever-hungry mouths of their offspring. Birds, in particular, often choose the oddest spots for their nests, from old vacuum cleaners and empty paint cans to mailboxes and aircraft. One mallard duck even built her nest in a window box on the seventh floor of an apartment building. She had to rely on a human helper to carry her ducklings down to the lake below. Urban birds make use of some unusual nesting materials, such as potato chip bags, plastic balls, tennis rackets, and telephone wire. Wasps also build their nests in awkward places, such as porches, greenhouses, and even under beds.

TROUSER NEST

A pair of pants provides a handy nesting place for a wren, which has a brood of hungry youngsters to feed (*right*). Birds that are willing to nest close to people can exploit nest sites that other competitors may not be bold enough to use. The presence of people may deter some predators from attacking the nest and stealing the young.

UGLY DUCKLINGS

A subdivision was built near the breeding grounds of this swan (*left*), so it now has to take its cygnets across pavement instead of grass to get to water. Mute swans usually have four to seven young gray cygnets, which cannot fly until they are four and a half months old. In the Middle Ages swan meat, especially that of fully grown cygnets, was highly prized as a source of food. Enormous numbers were eaten at royal banquets. At Christmas in 1251, King Henry III of England collected 125 swans for the festive celebration.

SNAKE INCUBATORS

Grass snakes often lay their eggs in garden compost piles (*right*). The warmth given off by the rotting vegetation makes the compost pile a natural incubator, which helps the embryos in the eggs develop fast enough to survive their first winter. Grass snakes have been known to lay their eggs also in manure heaps, piles of sawdust, and holes in the walls of bakeries, whose ovens keep the building very warm.

EGG CARRIER

The male midwife toad (*left*), found in Western European gardens and quarries, is a particularly caring parent. He winds a string of 35–50 eggs around his back legs and carries them around for protection. He keeps the eggs moist by dipping them in shallow pools or puddles from time to time. After about three weeks, the male takes his egg string into water, where the eggs hatch into tadpoles, which will develop into adult toads.

ILLUMINATED NEST

This house sparrow (*right*) has made its nest in a streetlight in Bahrain. Sparrows build untidy cupped or round nests of grass and straw lined with feathers. They often rob other birds, such as pigeons or ducks, of their feathers. Female sparrows lay four or five whitish eggs, often in other sparrows' nests. Two or three broods a year are normal, but four or five broods are possible. Eggs are incubated for about two weeks, and it may take another two weeks or so for the hatched nestlings to fledge, or become capable of flight. Some young nestlings fall out of their nests onto pavement below before they are able to fly.

BLOWING BUBBLES

Spittlebugs are insects that suck sap from plants. They are also known as froghoppers, from the way the nymphs, or larvae, hop about like tiny frogs. Adults can fly away from danger, but nymphs cannot, so they protect themselves by living in blobs of white froth ("spittle"), which they make by blowing air into a sticky fluid that comes out of their rear end (*left*). The froth also helps keep the nymph from drying out.

DISCOVERING URBAN WILDLIFE

ROADSIDE REFUGES

Grassy areas along the shoulders of roads and highways can become useful miniature nature refuges if the grass and flowers are allowed to grow. This Texas roadside (*above*) is filled with wild flowers, which attract insects, and the insects, in turn, attract birds. Small mammals, such as mice and voles, can feed on seeds, roots, and shoots in such grassy areas. Although the animals have to put up with traffic fumes and noise, they are not usually disturbed by people whizzing past in their cars, who are unaware of the living world so near their tires.

P eople have been living in cities for only a few thousand years, so this is a relatively new habitat for wildlife. But, unlike other wildlife habitats, it is growing rapidly. By some estimates, about 60 percent of the world's people will be living in towns and cities by the year 2020. We need to understand more about how urban animals survive if we want to encourage those animals that cause us no harm and control those that do. When we encourage urban animals to live in our towns and cities, it is inevitable that some popular species, such as birds and butterflies, will be eaten by unpopular ones, such as magpies and toads. This is all part of the balance of nature, even in an artificial urban setting. The four best ways to help urban animals are to provide shelter, homes, food, and water. Water is vital, both during summer droughts and winter frosts, and can be as small as a pan of water on a balcony or as large as a pond in a garden or city park.

FREE FOOD

These rainbow lorikeets (*right*) are feeding in a backyard in eastern Australia. People who feed birds in their gardens help them survive and are rewarded by wonderful close-up views of the birds. In countries colder than Australia, free food in the backyard or garden can be a real lifesaver in the winter, especially for small birds that need to eat a lot of food to keep warm.

BEE USEFUL

Some people in smaller towns keep bees in their gardens. This beekeeper (*left*) is checking on the well-being of the honeybees in one of his hives. Bees are excellent for gardens, as they pollinate flowers while collecting nectar and pollen to feed their larvae. Back in the hive, they change the nectar into honey, which the beekeeper can harvest.

FINDING OUT MORE

To plan the best conservation measures, it is important to know which animals are visiting our urban habitat, how many there are, and where they are living. Then any changes in populations can be noted, problems avoided, and help given to animals where it is most needed. Information gathered by ordinary people who identify the birds on their streets and in their gardens (*right*) can be very useful to conservationists. But it is unnecessary, and harmful, to catch the birds! A pair of binoculars and a good bird book are all a birdwatcher needs.

CLEARING UP

Many empty areas in cities, even small ones, can provide valuable habitats for wild animals, but only if unpolluted. These children (*left*) are clearing up a wild patch of ground in London, England, to make it safe for wildlife. But making things too neat and tidy both disturbs and discourages wild animals. Overgrown nooks and corners with piles of old logs and stones provide ideal places for animals to rest and hibernate. The greater the variety of native plants, including weeds, the greater the variety of insects and birds that can feed and shelter there.

FEEDING BIRDS

If you decide to feed the birds, try to use a variety of foods, such as peanuts, sunflower seeds, millet, cheese, pieces of fruit, suet, half coconuts, and bread crusts. You can offer food in different ways – such as on a table for starlings, in a hanging container for woodpeckers, and on the ground for thrushes. A variety of types of feeders are available on the market, but many people choose to make their own. It is a good idea to use a number of different places for the feeding stations. This makes it more difficult for cats to attack and gives the less aggressive birds a chance to feed. It also helps prevent the buildup of stale food, which might attract rats.

HERE ARE DIFFERENT TYPES OF BIRD FEEDERS YOU CAN MAKE YOURSELF:

1 Half a coconut
2 Peanuts or birdseed in a bottle or net
3 Peanuts hung on string or wire
4 Peanuts or suet in holes in a log
5 Pinecone filled with melted suet

FOR FURTHER INFORMATION

*The followng are some of the sources available that can help you find
out more about wildlife in urban areas.*

Books

Hanson, Jonathan. *There's a Bobcat in My Backyard: Living With and Enjoying Urban Wildlife*. Arizona-Sonora Desert Museum Guides series (University of Arizona)

Hodgkins, Fran. *Animals Among Us: Living With Suburban Wildlife* (Linnet)

Johnson, Catherine J., and others. *Welcoming Wildlife to the Garden: Creating Backyard and Balcony Habitats for Wildlife* (Hartley & Marks)

Lopez, Andrea Dawn. *When Raccoons Fall Through Your Ceiling: The Handbook for Coexisting With Wildlife*. Practical Guide series (University of North Texas)

Mizejewski, David. *Attracting Birds, Butterflies and Backyard Wildlife* (Creative Homeowner)

Peterson, Roger Tory (editor). *Peterson First Guide to Urban Wildlife*. Peterson First Guides series (Houghton Mifflin)

Roth, Sally. *The Backyard Bird Feeder's Bible: The A-to-Z Guide to Feeders, Seed Mixes, Projects and Treats* (Rodale)

Stump, Shelley, and Diana Landau (editors). *Living With Wildlife: How to Enjoy, Cope With, and Protect North America's Wild Creatures Around Your Home and Theirs* (Sierra Club)

Web sites

Backyard Nature www.backyardnature.net/

Birdwatchin.com www.birdwatchin.com/

Humane Society of the United States www.hsus.org/wildlife/urban_wildlife_our_wild_neighbors/

National Audubon Society www.audubon.org/bird/at%5Fhome/

National Wildlife Federation www.nwf.org/backyardwildlifehabitat/

U.S. Natural Resources Conservation Service www.nrcs.usda.gov/feature/backyard/

Virginia Department of Game and Inland Fisheries
    www.dgif.state.va.us/wildlife/habitat_at_home/index.html

Publisher's note to educators and parents: Our editors have carefully reviewed these Web sites to ensure that they are suitable for children. Many Web sites change frequently, however, and we cannot guarantee that a site's future contents will continue to meet our high standards of quality and educational value. Be advised that children should be closely supervised whenever they access the Internet.

Museums and urban wildlife reserves

American Museum of Natural History
Central Park West at 79th Street
New York, NY 10024

Don Edwards San Francisco Bay National Wildlife Refuge
Newark, CA

The Field Museum
1400 S. Lake Shore Drive
Chicago, IL 60605-2496

Golden Gate National Recreation Area
San Francisco, CA

Jamaica Bay Wildlife Refuge (Gateway National Recreation Area)
Brooklyn/Queens, NY

National Museum of Natural History
10th Street and Constitution Avenue, NW
Washington, DC 20560

Rocky Mountain Arsenal National Wildlife Refuge
Commerce City, CO

Russell W. Peterson Wildlife Refuge
Wilmington, DE

GLOSSARY

amphibians: a group of vertebrates that spend their life partly on land and partly in water, such as frogs and toads

bacteria: a group of single-celled microorganisms that lack a distinct cell nucleus; some bacteria cause disease

clutch: a group; often used to refer to the group of eggs hatched by certain animals at one time

cygnet: a young swan

echolocation: a method used by bats to detect the presence of objects; it makes use of echoes of sounds made by the bat and is similar to the underwater sonar system used by ships

ecosystem: a group of interdependent living things along with the environment they inhabit; a pond and the organisms living in it could be said to form an ecosystem

embryo: the early form of a living creature, before it is born or hatches

feral: referring to an animal that was, or whose ancestors were, domesticated but is now wild; for example, common rock pigeons are sometimes called feral pigeons because many are thought to be descended from domesticated pigeons

incubator: an apparatus that maintains conditions conducive for the development of something; for example, an incubator might be used to hatch eggs artificially

invertebrate: an animal without a backbone

larva: a young form of an animal; larvae (as the plural form is spelled) are usually quite different from adults in form – for example, the larva of a moth or butterfly is a caterpillar

mammals: a group of vertebrates that nourish their young on milk produced by the mother

marsupials: a group of mammals whose young are born at an early stage of development and then continue to mature while carried in a pouch on the mother's body; most modern marsupials are found in Australia and nearby islands

migration: the movement of animals from one environmental region to another, usually for purposes of breeding or feeding; some animals' migration journeys may cover thousands of miles, but most are shorter

nymph: a larva of certain insects; the nymph looks somewhat similar to an adult and does not pass through a pupa stage as it matures

pupa: a stage in the development of certain insects, during which larvae are transformed into adults; insects in the pupal stage typically lie within a cocoon or similar protective case

rodents: a group of small mammals with large front "incisor" teeth that are good for gnawing; members of the group include beavers, mice, rats, and squirrels

thermal: a column of warm rising air

vertebrate: an animal with a backbone

INDEX